**Dealing with a Depressed Loved One:**

**You're Not Alone**

**Terrence C.J. Ferguson**

**Published by:**

**Empowerment in Knowledge**
**P.O. Box 4481**
**Kettering, MD 20774**



**Published in the United States of America**

## DEDICATION

**This book is dedicated to my loving family: Lawrence J., Carlene, Lawrence D., Eve, Trina, Christian, Emerald, and Lillian. I cannot omit my loving extended family as well, all of the Fergusons and Swinneys. I love you all! These loved ones have supported me all of my life. Thank you so much for all of your love and support. Without you this book would not be in existence.**

## EPIGRAPH

**When dealing with a depressed loved one, remember them as they were and not as who they are now. Remember the special times you had together, not the rough times that you face today and may face in the future. Remember that if it were you who were depressed, your family members would do all they could to help you, so why not do for them what you know they would do for you.**

**– Terrence Ferguson**

## TABLE OF CONTENTS

## Warning – Disclaimer

**This book is designed to provide help for people dealing with a loved one who is suffering with clinical depression. It is sold with the understanding that the author is not an authority in this field but rather is sharing what he has experienced personally. If expert help is needed, an expert in this field should be contacted. You are encouraged to learn all that you can from the different resources that are available on this topic. A few resources have been included in this book, which can hopefully help you. Every effort has been made to make this book as helpful to you as possible. This book should only be used as information from one person to another and not as an authority on this topic. This book contains information that is current only up to the print date. The author shall have neither liability nor responsibility to any person or entity with respect to any loss or damage caused, or alleged to have been caused, directly or indirectly, by the information that is in this book. If you do not wish to be bound by the above, you may return this book to the publisher for a full refund.**

## INTRODUCTION

"Why my loved one? Why me? I'm just a child. I'm not supposed to deal with this kind of stuff yet." These were some of the thoughts going through my head. In actuality I was not a child, I was twenty-three years old and just coming out of graduate school. I was recently engaged to get married and everything seemed to be falling into place in my life. There was one thing that seemed to be out of order around this time, however. For whatever reason, things were not quite right with one of my loved ones.

**It doesn't matter who the loved one was, all that matters is that this person was important to me. Although this loved one is real, in order to conceal the person's identity, I will refer to the person as James. For a while I was frustrated with the people at James's job and even people at James's church. After talking to a dear friend, I decided that it was time to do some research on what might be going on with James. My research led me to study signs and symptoms of clinical depression and the rest was history. It was scary to think that James was depressed.**

**I thought, "How could God allow this to happen?" This person was one of the most righteous people that I knew. James was truly a prayer warrior. James was God's child. You never focus on some issues until it happens to you or someone who you know. Throughout the process of trying to help James, there have been good and bad times. Through our journey, yes our journey, I have learned a lot. What I have learned in this process is that if someone is struggling with depression, it really does affect the people around him or her, if those people choose to walk alongside through that tough period of the**

**person's life. I, along with several other people that I love, chose to walk alongside James during this tough time.**

**That decision has been the difference between James's life and potential death.**

# CHAPTER 1
# WHO DO I TURN TO?

Once I realized that something was not quite right with James, I tried to think of who I could turn to. There was no easy answer to this question. For starters, I had no clue what was wrong. I heard what James would say and I took it to be the truth because I was hearing it from someone I loved. Initially when I would hear that various people were mistreating James, I naturally got upset, although there was not much that I could do. I started talking to one of my good friends who was a psychology major and this

**friend suggested that I do some research on the matter. My friend suggested that I look into symptoms of depression because this friend had dealt with some similar issues with someone who the friend loved and cared about. Around this time, I tried to think of who in my family I could talk to. I couldn't really talk to James about what I was feeling because I didn't want to upset him. I figured that James would not want me to talk to too many people who knew about what was going on. From the people who I regularly came in contact with, clinical depression seemed to be a topic that was not discussed at all.**

**This is possibly true of the African-American community in general, although that is just a personal thought of mine. I think it is even worse in the Christian community because it may be thought that we should be able to pray our problems away. Yes, prayer is powerful, and God has given us that ability to communicate with Him, but I also know that clinical depression is real and some sort of action is needed as well. For years, I have expressed a desire to bring clinical depression to the forefront of conversations and people's awareness in general.**

I think awareness in this area, will at least educate people about symptoms of clinical depression and some possible solutions for healing. That is one of my motivations for writing this book. I want to help others who may be going through a similar situation as I went through. In regard to looking for others to open up to about this situation, I did not think I could open up to anyone at my church because I was not sure what any of the church members I knew could do, other than pray for James and me. I did request prayers from a few people without going into any significant details.

**I started to think of this as a problem that I personally had to deal with, along with James and a few other family members and friends.**

## CHAPTER 2
## THINGS ARE GETTING CLEARER

It took some time to follow up on my friend's advice of doing research on depression. Once I completed my research, I determined that James indeed was depressed. This was both a scary revelation and a relief at the same time. The revelation was scary because I had no clue what was involved with clinical depression. I knew that depressed people were people who were sad, but I had no clue what clinical depression was really like. I did not know what to expect from James either.

**I knew that he would never do anything to hurt me intentionally, but at the same time we certainly were not on the same page in our thought processes. The revelation was a relief because I knew for sure what we were dealing with and I could do further research in order to determine how to help James deal with this undiagnosed depressed state. I would spend the next several years doing research and trying to find different solutions to this problem. One problem that I faced was that depression is a topic that is not widely discussed, at least in the community that I live in.**

**I have a feeling that this lack of communication on this issue is not limited to my community. Now that I and a few other people knew what the problem was, the question now was, "How do we fix this depressed person?" Unfortunately, there were no standard operating procedures readily available to tell us what to do. For a while the few of us trying to help James tried to understand and sympathize with him. We tried reasoning with James, but no matter what we tried, James simply did not see things the way that we saw them. It was like James was living in another world. Another problem**

that I was facing was the fact that James lived alone, and because of that there was no one around on a consistent basis to hold him accountable for his actions. The few of us trying to help James found out that he had stopped going to his doctor appointments because he did not like what the doctors were saying. This was dangerous as well because without attending any of the doctor appointments, there was no professional evaluating the situation.

In addition to that, none of the prescriptions that the doctor had previously prescribed were being taken.

**The choice of taking the medication prescribed was tough because I read some of the side effects of the medication and some of those effects seemed worse than some of the symptoms the medicine was needed for. One of the medications (I can't remember which one it was) cited that it "might" make the user more suicidal and forgetful. The same medication required the patient to wear a sign indicating that you are taking the medication and not to go out in the sun while taking the medication. In all reality, if I had been given this medication, I might not have wanted to take it either.**

**In spite of all of that, I along with the other helpers tried to encourage James to go back to the doctor, but he would refuse. In the midst of the depression, it seemed like James's health was also starting to fail. I believe this was a direct result of what the depression was doing to him. Over the course of several years, yes several years, the helpers and I had to take James to the hospital a few times a year. These just weren't typical trips to the hospital. These were emergency visits in which James sometimes seemed like he was facing a life and death situation. In the first few years when we started taking**

**James to the hospital, he was diagnosed with diabetes. So not only did James have to deal with depression, but now he also had to deal with diabetes. James would let the diabetes go unchecked for long stretches of time, and as a result of this, his blood sugar levels would go through the roof. One time when we called an ambulance, the measuring device could not even read the blood sugar level because it was so high.**

**James's family and friends thought that one day he would go into a diabetic coma because the blood sugar level would be at such dangerous levels. In James's fragile**

**mental state, he said that he did not care about the consequences of letting his diabetes go unchecked. At this point it had become clear that it would be almost impossible to "fix" James, but we could not give up on him. We continued to support him although it hurt to see him in this condition. We had faith and hope that one day God would completely heal James.**

## CHAPTER 3
## OPENING UP THE BOTTLE

**I'm not sure when it happened, but somewhere along the way I started to share more about what I was going through in dealing with a depressed loved one. This was a monumental progression for me. For those who knew me growing up, one of the things that people would say to me is that I smiled "ALL OF THE TIME." For the most part, this was true. I did not feel comfortable sharing my feelings with people when I was a child. I had a good life growing up, but I had disappointments as well, just like anyone**

**else. I learned to bottle up my emotions, and when people asked me how I was doing, it was always "fine" or "good." How many people know that things are not ALWAYS "fine" or "good"? I think the right people were in my life at the right time to allow me to start opening up the bottle and let my feelings out. Through sharing my feelings and what I was going through, I was able to deal with caring for James even better. No, nothing changed, but I was able to feel like someone cared about me and the situation that I was in. Strangely enough, I was also able to help several other people I encountered who**

**were going through a similar situation with their loved ones. For some reason, I think I was like many other people initially. I did not want to share with anyone that someone I loved was clinically depressed because I felt it was a private matter. Now I am relieved that I started sharing what I was going through with other people because my family received help, but I was also able to provide comfort and support to others throughout the process as well.**

## CHAPTER 4
## KEEPING YOURSELF AND YOUR FAMILY SAFE

It was difficult for me to write this chapter because it feels wrong to say that you need to protect your family from someone that you love. However, it is still important to note that in the midst of helping a loved one who is dealing with depression, you have to make sure that your family is safe. I know without a shadow of a doubt that James would never intentionally hurt me or my family, emotional, physically, or otherwise. However, I also am not an expert on clinical depression.

**I don't know what someone in a depressed state is capable of. The main thing that I needed to do was to set boundaries when it came to my family. When James was in a good place mentally and emotionally, I did not have to have too many boundaries; however, when I sensed that things were not as they should have been at that point I had to make sure that my family felt safe. In order to ensure the safety of my family, I frequently would deal with James on a one-on-one basis. I would also make my request known so that James knew where I was coming from.**

**At one point in time, James would just show up at my house, and I did not think that, that was appropriate. So I would ask him if he could call me first if he wanted to visit, and I would let him know if it was OK for a visit. I would also visit James on a regular basis so that he knew I cared about him, but this also allowed me to deal with James on my terms. I have also talked to a few other people in the past several years about this very issue. The difference with one of the individuals who I talked to was that this person's loved one who was dealing with depression was living in this person's**

house. The loved one who was depressed expressed erratic behaviors on several occasions and there were young children in the house who were intimidated by these actions. As a result of this, the family members in the house had to resort to locking their bedroom doors at night, and eventually they had to ask their loved one to leave. They still visited their loved one, but having the loved one live with them was not working out for everyone involved. Sometimes we have to make tough decisions to make sure that everyone is comfortable and safe.

**Just because our loved ones don't live with us does not mean that we cannot have a positive influence on their lives. I feel that I have had a significantly positive impact on James's life. It is easy for me to love him and help him because I am confident that he would do the same thing for me. There are no hard and fast rules to keeping your family safe. You just have to use common sense. If the person does not exhibit intimidating behaviors, there is more likely less that you have to worry about. However, if there are things that are happening that raise your antenna, you may want to pay close attention to**

**your loved one. You need to see if any changes are needed in how you and your family are interacting with your loved one.**

## CHAPTER 5

## You cannot consume yourself with the problem. If you break down too, you won't be good for anyone.

If you are anything like me, it may be hard not to constantly focus on your sick loved one. I thought about James and his situation all of the time. As a man, I thought I could fix this person. I saw a problem and wanted to find a solution. As I told James on many occasions, it was like he was in another world. Did I want to give up on the situation sometimes? Yes! Did I get upset and frustrated at times? Yes! Did I get down sometimes? Absolutely!

**Things got to the point where I was becoming more and more unhappy because it was becoming harder to deal with the situation. I cried so much over the period of a few years that I couldn't cry anymore. I was not becoming good for anyone. Not my family, James, my community, or even myself. This was affecting the relationship that I had with his wife, and it was affecting me in general. At some points in the situation, I did not look forward to going to see James because I could not really visit. Constantly, I, along with a few other people, had to clean up after James and**

make sure that he was alright. We also had to make sure that he did not need to go to the hospital. Those of us who were helping also had to make sure that he had enough food in the house. It was also difficult for me to listen to James's paranoia, even about some of the people that I loved and a few times about myself. Even knowing that James was depressed, it was still hard to hear his thoughts about me being against him too. Things seemed to get harder and harder, and after a while I just felt pretty low. Once I realized that I may have been slightly depressed, I suggested that my wife and I go on a mini-

**vacation. After the trip, I felt great. Those small getaways meant the world to my health and overall well-being. I realized that if I allowed myself to get depressed I would not be good for anyone including himself. I had to start taking time out for myself, and you need to do the same thing. Yes you! The situation will still be there when you get back. So the lesson that I learned in this case was to take a break.**

**When I take out time for myself, I can deal with the situation and everything else that life has to offer a lot better.**

## CHAPTER 6
## Helpful information from some loving people changed my life!

When things had gotten to a low point in James's life, I was at a loss as of what to do. I was one of the few people at the time that James could talk to, and I wanted to give him some sound information. I did not want to give advice that would be counterproductive to James's situation. I had begun to regularly talk to a trusted friend during this time.

**This individual had been a social worker before and this person was a great listening ear for a long period of time.**

**I will never forget how much this friend meant to me. Although this friend couldn't take away my frustration or sense of failure, I will always be grateful to this person for being a listening ear to me. It was exactly what I needed during that time. After listening to my dilemma for a while, this friend suggested that James should go to an assisted living facility. I thought to myself, assisted living, what in the world is that?**

**Some other very thoughtful people had mentioned the same thing to a few more of the people trying to help James during this time. It took about a year of asking James if he would visit some of these assisted living facilities with me before he gave it a second thought. James did not mind visiting assisted living facilities with me because we always seemed to come around at meal time. As a result of this, we frequently received free meals. In addition to that, assisted living facilities provide entertainment to their residents, so James and I were able to see many entertainment acts as well during our**

**visits. Over time, James softened up to the idea of assisted living, and eventually he said that he tried it his way for a LONG time and it didn't get him too far. So now he wanted to try to listen to some of his friends and family. After making the decision to move into an assisted living facility, the relationship that I now have with James is awesome. We can actually visit with one another instead of me having to do a lot of house maintenance type work. I am a strong believer in assisted living after seeing James go through the process.**

**All of this took place because some kind people shared powerful information with me and a few other people that I know. This information changed my life and James's life.**

**I am happy that this solution turned out to be a great fit for James and his family and friends. Everything still is not perfect, and I would be lying if I said that it was. On the other hand, James is safe and receiving good attention and care on a daily basis. This has also allowed me to really enjoy my time with James.**

**I am no longer overwhelmed with trying to help him maintain his household while trying to help maintain my own household at the same time.**

**If you would like to learn more about my experience with assisted living, please feel free to contact me.**

## CHAPTER 7

## Pray! It really works! Do the best you can do and leave the rest up to God.

One of the greatest lessons that I learned from this entire ordeal is that, as a man, I cannot fix everything. I wanted to fix James for years, and it took me years to figure out that I just could not fix him. This was a God-sized task, and only God could heal James. In addition to this, only God could allow me and the other people helping James to be at peace with the situation. I learned that I needed to continue to support James, but I also needed to do A LOT OF PRAYING! I have never prayed so much in all of y life.

There was nothing else that I could do. Yes, I could be helpful and be an encourager, but in my own strength, I could not take the depression away. I thank God for allowing me to see James whole again. This was one of the greatest miracles that I have witnessed in my thirty-three years on this Earth. Words cannot describe how happy I was to see the life returned to James. I knew that this was only possible through God. All in all, James is doing great, and I am so glad that God allowed me to see this miraculous outcome. My family and friends have had a happy outcome, and I

**hope that you and your friends and family will have a similar outcome as well. Please continue to get knowledge, and don't stop praying. I want to encourage all of you who are out there caring for another person, and please remember that there is power in prayer and empowerment in knowledge!**

## CHAPTER 8
## RESOURCES

### Tip # 1
### Accept all of the help that you can get.

It is common to want to hide what is going on with a depressed loved one in your life. The reality is that by sharing your story with others and accepting their help, you can have a better quality of life as well as your loved one. I personally never would have learned about assisted living if I had never shared my story with others and accepted the help I was offered.

### Tip # 2
### Look into alternatives before things get bad. You don't want to wait until the last minute and make a quick decision.

There is a saying that I've heard most of my life that says, "The early bird catches the worm." I think that is true when it comes to senior care as well. I don't think that we should react when something goes wrong. I think we should have a plan in place in case things go bad. Do your due diligence. Research resources that can help, and even look into facilities that can help if you and your family are unable to take care of your loved one.

### Tip # 3
### Research any place you are considering moving your loved one into. Talk to the residents, families of residents, and staff.

This is a continuation of tip # 2. As you're researching resources and facilities, the best thing you can do is get an accurate picture of what you would be dealing with. Talk to customers of the resources and see if they are happy with the result of the products and services. Talk to the residents of the facilities and see how they are treated, what the food is like, what the response times are like, etc. Talk to the staff about their views of the facility and services, and certainly talk to family members about what they have observed. Also, you might be able to get a good picture of what is going on simply by doing a search online.

**Tip # 4**
**Encourage your loved one to get long-term care insurance.**

**A lot of people still may not know about long-term care insurance, but it can literally save you millions of dollars in the long run. It also puts you in the driver seat on what kind of care you will receive. Do you or your loved one want to decide what kind of help he or she receive, or does he or she want to put his or her future in the hands of family or sometimes even strangers?**

**Tip # 5**
**Take a break!**

**There came a time in my life when I thought I NEED TO TAKE A BREAK! I realized that if I didn't slow down and stop trying to solve every problem for my loved one and worry about him constantly, I would burn myself out. If I burned out, I wouldn't be good for my loved one, my family, my community, and myself. Please take a break, and do some things that you enjoy doing.**

**Tip # 6**
**Talk to seniors about what they want before they need help.**

**I believe it is important to get input from seniors early. Before the senior needs assistance ask, him or her what he or she would like to do once he or she needs help in everyday life functions. Some seniors will want to stay home while others may want to go to a facility.**

**Tip # 7**
**Make sure that the loved one's legal matters are in order. You want your loved one to make a rational decision (wills, trusts, POA, etc.).**

**If at all possible, another thing that you should do is to make sure that your family member or friend's legal matters are in order. It is much better to get things settled when the person is in his or her right mind than to wait until later and possibly get nothing in place.**

**Tip # 8**

**Get support for yourself! A support group could be a great resource for you personally.**

A lot of times caregivers spend a lot of time and energy supporting the loved one. It is easy to overlook the fact that the caregiver needs to be supported as well. There are several very good support groups out there, and if you are not interested in support group then surround yourself with people who can be there for you.

**Tip # 9**

**Look into financial sources your loved one may qualify for.**

There are a number of financial resources available to senior citizens, but you will never know whether the senior in your life qualifies or not if you don't look into those resources and appropriately apply for the benefits. There are Social Security benefits, state benefits, federal benefits,

**veteran benefits, and a host of other resources that the senior in your life may qualify for. Check them all out; it is certainly worth the time and effort.**

## FINAL THOUGHT

**I really do hope that this book has helped someone. I am still working with James and plan to continue to do so, because he means that much to me.**

www.ingramcontent.com/pod-product-compliance
Ingram Content Group UK Ltd.
Pitfield, Milton Keynes, MK11 3LW, UK
UKHW051135260726
13967UKWH00010B/3057

9 781257 419678